CARES?

A Guided Self-Help &
Devotional Journal for
the Seasons of Life

God Has Great
Plans For You's

Dr. Melissa Murray-Cary

Who
CARES?

A Guided Self-Help & Devotional Journal for the Seasons of Life

*"To everything
there is a season,
A time for every purpose
under heaven."*
(Ecclesiastes 3:1 NKJV)

Dr. Melita J. Murray-Carney

XULON PRESS ELITE

Xulon Press
2301 Lucien Way #415
Maitland, FL 32751
407.339.4217
www.xulonpress.com

This book may be purchased in bulk to promote health and wellness in corporate or educational settings and faith-based organizations. Please contact Xulon Press Book Sales Department at 1-866-909-2665 or email us at whocaresjournal@gmail.com.

This book is intended to provide helpful information on the subjects discussed and not intended as a substitute for medical advice. For diagnosis or treatment of any medical or psychological problem, please consult your physician or mental health professional. The author and publisher are not responsible for any negative consequences of following the suggestions or information in this book.

Unless otherwise indicated, Scripture quotations are taken from the New King James Version (NKJV). Copyright © 1982 by Thomas Nelson, Inc. Used by permission. All rights reserved.

Cover image used under license from Shutterstock.

Paperback ISBN-13: 978-1-6628-1690-1
Hard Cover ISBN-13: 978-1-6628-1691-8
Ebook ISBN-13: 978-1-6628-1692-5

This journal belongs to:

_____

CONTENTS

ACKNOWLEDGEMENTS

Dear Heavenly Father,
Thank You for inspiring wisdom and guidance in writing this SIP (Spiritual, Inspirational, Psychological) journal. Most of all, thank you for using me to assist others in finding their true purpose through a holistic perspective on self-care.

Special Thanks:
In memory of my late father, Dr. Winston C. Murray, who was an author, educator, politician, and the one who gently reminded me that the culmination of a doctoral degree was to publish a book. I will be eternally grateful to have had a dad who was my icon.

To my mother, Dr. Alice Murray Jamison, a retired counseling psychologist and superb grant writer. Thank you for paving the psychological trail and for helping me have a successful career.

In memory of my late maternal grandmother, Mrs. Josephine B. Hargrett, who was a great educator and provided me with inspiration and a strong spiritual foundation. I will be forever grateful to have had a grandmother who believed in me and propelled me to fulfill my dreams.

To my siblings and bonus children, Aisha, Sir Otiato, Cheree, Tracee, Schulyer, Irvin, Michelle, Lamont, Raymond IV, and Jasmine. Thank you for your love and support.

To my brilliant husband, Raymond A. Carney III, who encouraged me to be my authentic self and who was determined to navigate the stormy patches of married life with me rather than give up. Thank you for your love and commitment.

Last but definitely not least: to family members, friends, and church members who are authors, editors, poets, and bloggers; you modeled the power of words and gave me the inspiration to complete this journal. Thank you!

PREFACE

MY RELATIONSHIP WITH JOURNALING BEGAN WITH Oprah Winfrey. I loved hearing about her gratitude entries and soon found the same love and appreciation she had for them.

But what began as a calming activity of appreciation and edification soon became a coping mechanism that I used to keep myself from sinking into a growing sea of sadness, anxiety, and frustration. My marriage was crumbling, and I was inundated with emotional stress.

For the first time in what was then seven years of marriage, my husband and I deteriorated into finger-pointing, lashing out, hurting each other, and seeing each other as enemies instead of life partners.

I was overwhelmed. I struggled with maintaining optimism and a positive mindset. Yes, even as a licensed clinical psychologist, I was in a state of emotional crisis.

However, through my love for and trust in God, I still found the strength to journal. Journaling became a safe haven for sharing my true feelings, releasing my negative emotions, and working through my marital challenges.

I always ended my journal entries believing that God knew my circumstances, and I trusted in His promise that "I will never leave you nor forsake you" (Hebrews 13:5 NKJV*).

Through it all (and remaining married), I conquered my emotional distress, strengthened my faith, and I never stopped journaling.

Journaling worked for me, and it can work for you too!

---

* All Scripture verses are taken from the NKJV

Additionally, the scientific community is in complete agreement that writing is a useful and comforting means of expressing emotions.[1] Furthermore, expressive or therapeutic writing has been shown to improve psychological well-being and enhance physical functioning.[2]

The bottom line is that journaling is a powerful and valuable tool for promoting and enhancing mental, emotional, physical, and spiritual wellness.

In conclusion, I dedicate this Spiritual, Inspirational, and Psychological (SIP) self-help and devotional journal to the following:

To those who have no health insurance and therefore have little or no access to mental health services.

To the pastor, minister, or chaplain that bears the burden of caring for others and feels alone with their pain.

To the individual who lived in foster care or was adopted, but still has feelings of abandonment.

To the Christian believer that doubts the healing properties of psychotherapy.

I acknowledge these individuals because the struggle in seeking and getting help is real in all walks of life.

My prayer for you is that this journal will help you achieve whole health through reflection, affirmation, spiritual confirmation, and gentle reminders.

I chose to refer to each chapter as seasons because we experience transitional periods in our lives that parallel the seasons of the year. Just like the leaves change from summer to fall, our life seasons undergo transitions that impact our mind, body, and spirit. Please consider starting with the season that is most relevant or interesting to you.

Also, I have included my unique collection of cloud images because clouds represent God's covering and divine presence (Exodus 13:21).

It's easy to allow a cloud of darkness to hover over your mind. But imagine for a moment a journey in the clouds, where you feel a sense of peace and safety because of God's presence around you. Linger for a while and talk to God. Enjoy his presence and begin to feel your dark cloud floating away. Then, when you are ready, return revived and refreshed to the world of journaling.

From my heart to yours,

Dr. Melita

Season 1

NEW BEGINNINGS

It's scary sometimes to attempt something new, but if you don't try, you will never know whether you can accomplish the task. So, let today be your NEW beginning. Let's start by writing down your goals.

Reflection: **What are some of your goals?**

_____

_____

_____

_____

_____

Affirmation: **All things are possible!**

Confirmation: **"Whatever you ask the Father in My name He may give you." John 15:16**

_____

_____

_____

_____

_____

Take one day at a time with your goals. Divide your goals into small, manageable parts, and enjoy what you have accomplished after each smaller step.[1] Tomorrow will take care of itself.

Reflection: **What goals seem overwhelming and need to be divided into smaller, more manageable parts?**

_____

_____

_____

_____

_____

Affirmation: **Set achievable goals!**

_____

_____

_____

_____

_____

_____

_____

_____

When we make time to think through a problem, we can more readily devise an answer. There may be times when you need assistance, but that's part of the solution.

Reflection: **What problems are you facing that require more time to resolve? What are some possible solutions that come to mind?**

_____

_____

_____

_____

_____

Affirmation: **I'm a problem-solver!**

Confirmation: **"I can do all things through Christ who strengthens me." Philippians 4:13**

_____

_____

_____

_____

_____

_____

_____

PROVERBS 1:5
"A WISE MAN WILL HEAR AND INCREASE LEARNING, AND
A MAN OF UNDERSTANDING WILL ATTAIN WISE COUNSEL."

As you work on your goals, remember that your choices guide your life. You can fulfill your dreams when you fully embrace your desires.

Reflection: **What choices are you making to reach your goals?**

_____

_____

_____

_____

_____

Affirmation: **I envision my miracle!**

Confirmation: **"Yet I show you a more excellent way."
1 Corinthians 12:31**

_____

_____

_____

_____

_____

_____

_____

_____

Set realistic expectations for yourself. You are the only person who can stop you from achieving great things.

Reflection: **How do you plan to achieve realistic goals?**

_____

_____

_____

_____

_____

Affirmation: **I will be a high achiever!**

_____

_____

_____

_____

_____

_____

_____

_____

_____

_____

DEUTERONOMY 28:2
"AND ALL THESE BLESSINGS SHALL COME UPON YOU
AND OVERTAKE YOU, BECAUSE YOU OBEY THE VOICE
OF THE LORD YOUR GOD."

Set your own pace and be intentional and consistent. You may pause for a moment, but stay focused and keep working toward(s) your goals.

Reflection: **What is a reasonable pace for accomplishing your goals?**

_____

_____

_____

_____

_____

Affirmation: **I will stick to my goals today!**

Confirmation: **"But you, be strong and do not let your hands be weak, for your work shall be rewarded!" 2 Chronicles 15:7**

_____

_____

_____

_____

_____

_____

_____

_____

When you have been told that you are stupid and ugly, it is hard to see the first-rate version of yourself that lies within. However, you can shift the negative thoughts instilled in you by others by looking at yourself in the mirror and saying, "I am smart and beautiful," even when you have a hard time believing it.[2] Begin to love yourself and avoid comparing yourself with others. God created you to be unique!

Reflection: **In order to perceive yourself more positively, what do you need to do?**

_____

_____

_____

_____

_____

Affirmation: **I'm a first-rate version of myself!**

Confirmation: **"I am fearfully and wonderfully made." Psalm 139:14**

_____

_____

_____

_____

_____

_____

_____

Being popular generates great feelings, but is your popularity leading you down the right path? Standing up for what's right can be challenging when it lands you in the unpopular camp, but you will sleep well knowing you did the right thing.

Reflection: **What is your preference: being popular or doing what's right? What's influencing this preference?**

_____

_____

_____

_____

_____

Affirmation: **I will do what's right, even though it may not be popular!**

_____

_____

_____

_____

_____

_____

_____

_____

ACTS 2:17
**"YOUR YOUNG MEN SHALL SEE VISIONS, YOUR OLD MEN
SHALL DREAM DREAMS."**

Be your authentic self and be happy. No matter what you do, some people aren't going to like you—so why be one of them?

Reflection: **Who or what is preventing you from being your authentic self ?**

_____

_____

_____

_____

_____

Affirmation: **I will be true to me!**

Confirmation: **"May He grant you according to your heart's desire, and fulfill all your purpose." Psalm 20:4**

_____

_____

_____

_____

_____

_____

_____

_____

Your thoughts affect your feelings, and your feelings influence your behavior.[3] Identify your purpose and shape your life!

Reflection: **What role does your thinking play in your behavior and purpose in life?**

_____

_____

_____

_____

_____

Affirmation: **I have a purpose!**

Confirmation: **"I know that You can do everything, and that no purpose of Yours can be withheld from You." Job 42:2**

_____

_____

_____

_____

_____

_____

_____

Betrayals and mistakes are inevitable. Nevertheless, don't allow negative experiences to bring you down. Focus instead on the lessons you learned that would help you become a stronger and better person.

Reflection: **What lessons have you learned to improve your personal development?**

_____

_____

_____

_____

_____

Affirmation: **I can learn valuable lessons from a test!**

_____

_____

_____

_____

_____

_____

_____

_____

Getting sucked into negativity is easy. Keep positive people around you who inspire you to remain positive.

Reflection: **What is the best way to keep yourself in a positive bubble?**

_____

_____

_____

_____

Affirmation: **I will stay away from negativity!**

Confirmation: **"Evil company corrupts good habits."**
1 Corinthians 15:33

_____

_____

_____

_____

_____

_____

_____

ISAIAH 40:31
"BUT THOSE WHO WAIT ON THE LORD, SHALL RENEW THEIR STRENGTH."

Season 2

LOVE

WHEN YOU LOVE WHAT YOU DO, YOU RECEIVE much satisfaction from life and experience great success. Start loving what you do. You won't regret it.

Reflection: **What are you strongly passionate about right now?**

_____

_____

_____

_____

_____

Affirmation: **I will love what I do!**

Confirmation: **"And whatever you do, do it heartily, as to the Lord and not to men." Colossians 3:23**

_____

_____

_____

_____

_____

It's a great feeling when others love you despite your bad habits and attitudes. Show some love to somebody you dislike or who dislikes you, and watch for a change in their attitude.

Reflection: **Can you remember a time when you demonstrated love for someone who disliked you? How did it feel? What did you learn from this experience?**

_____

_____

_____

_____

Affirmation: **I will love the unlovable!**

_____

_____

_____

_____

_____

_____

_____

_____

You were born to be loved, and you deserve to be loved. Most importantly, God loves you! Allow yourself to be embraced by this loving thought!

Reflection: **What loving thoughts from God are warming your heart today?**

_____

_____

_____

_____

_____

Affirmation: **I will embrace God's love!**

Confirmation: **"Yes, I have loved you with an everlasting love . . . with lovingkindness I have drawn you." Jeremiah 31:3**

_____

_____

_____

_____

_____

_____

_____

PSALM 145:8
"THE LORD IS GRACIOUS AND FULL OF COMPASSION,
SLOW TO ANGER AND GREAT IN MERCY."

Let love rule your heart. Anger and fear only stunt your personal growth; by releasing fear and anger instead, you will be able to allow love to take residence within.

Reflection: **What is residing in your heart? Love or fear? What can you do to welcome love and eliminate anger and fear?**

_____

_____

_____

_____

_____

Affirmation: **Only love! No room for anger and fear!**

Confirmation: **"There is no fear in love; but perfect love casts out fear." 1 John 4:18**

_____

_____

_____

_____

_____

_____

_____

Love is a powerful emotion that shapes creativity!

Reflection: **In what ways does love shape your creativity? List three things you have created that were inspired by feelings of love.**

_____

_____

_____

_____

_____

Affirmation: **Let love flow!**

_____

_____

_____

_____

_____

_____

_____

_____

_____

_____

_____

_____

Love without reservations!

Reflection: **What prevents you from loving others unconditionally?**

_____

_____

_____

_____

_____

Affirmation: **I will love unconditionally!**

Confirmation: **"A new commandment I give to you, that you love one another; as I have loved you." John 13:34**

_____

_____

_____

_____

_____

_____

_____

_____

JOHN 15:13
"GREATER LOVE HAS NO ONE THAN THIS, THAN TO LAY
DOWN ONE'S LIFE FOR HIS FRIENDS."

Forgiveness isn't easy, but it is possible. Show some tender loving care, and your heart will be more open to forgiving.

Reflection: **What roadblocks keep you from loving difficult people?**

_____

_____

_____

_____

_____

Affirmation: **Forgiveness heals!**

Confirmation: **"Be kind to one another, tenderhearted, forgiving one another, even as God in Christ forgave you." Ephesians 4:32**

_____

_____

_____

_____

_____

_____

_____

_____

It's easy to take people for granted. Appreciate and cherish those you love.

Reflection: **Who are the people in your life you need to make more time to appreciate? How can you begin to show a greater appreciation for them?**

_____

_____

_____

_____

_____

Affirmation: **I will cherish my loved ones!**

_____

_____

_____

_____

_____

_____

_____

_____

GALATIANS 6:9
"AND LET US NOT GROW WEARY WHILE DOING GOOD, FOR IN DUE SEASON WE SHALL REAP IF WE DO NOT LOSE HEART."

Season 3

ANTICIPATION

WE OFTEN WISH GOD WOULD SAY YES TO ALL OF our desires, but He doesn't. We have to learn to trust Him when He says, "Not yet," and have faith that He is working out the situation for an outcome that will be in our favor. What a wonderful idea to embrace—that God has something better planned for you!

Reflection: **In what ways can you strengthen your faith in God?**

_____

_____

_____

_____

_____

Affirmation: **I will trust that God knows what's best for me!**

Confirmation: **"Is anything too hard for the Lord?" Genesis 18:14**

_____

_____

_____

_____

_____

When you have hope, you are motivated to do anything. Hope breeds optimism and drives you to fulfill your desires.

Reflection: **What helps you to be hopeful? How has hope made a difference in your life?**

_____

_____

_____

_____

Affirmation: **I am hopeful!**

_____

_____

_____

_____

_____

_____

_____

_____

When you are mindful that the unexpected will occur, it helps you anticipate greatness and cope with disappointments.

Reflection: **When unexpected events happen, how do you cope?**

_____

_____

_____

_____

_____

Affirmation: **I will expect the unexpected!**

Confirmation: **"I will go before you, and make the crooked places straight." Isaiah 45:2**

_____

_____

_____

_____

_____

_____

_____

_____

PHILIPPIANS 4:19
"AND MY GOD SHALL SUPPLY ALL YOUR NEED ACCORDING TO HIS RICHES IN GLORY BY CHRIST JESUS."

Choices and decisions pave a pathway for true purpose. Stay true to your calling!

Reflection: **What have you identified as your true calling?**

_____

_____

_____

_____

_____

Affirmation: **I will follow my true path!**

Confirmation: **"Then you will call upon Me and go and pray to Me, and I will listen to you." Jeremiah 29:12**

_____

_____

_____

_____

_____

_____

_____

_____

The mountains of difficulties we face in daily life can appear so insurmountable at times that it seems easier to give up. But if we take the road of patience and diligence, we can remove those mountains.

Reflection: **What are your mountains of difficulty? What is the key to overcoming your obstacles?**

_____

_____

_____

_____

_____

Affirmation: **I will be patient and diligent!**

Confirmation: **"Therefore, my beloved brethren, be steadfast, immovable . . . knowing that your labor is not in vain in the Lord." 1 Corinthians 15:58**

_____

_____

_____

_____

_____

_____

_____

There are some circumstances beyond your control, but you can control your attitude. It is often easier to entertain negative thoughts, which lead to a negative attitude, than positive ones. Next time you're facing a challenge, check your thoughts and attitude!

Reflection: **What helps keep your attitude in check?**

_____

_____

_____

_____

_____

Affirmation: **I will maintain a positive attitude no matter the circumstances!**

_____

_____

_____

_____

_____

_____

_____

_____

_____

ISAIAH 26:3
"YOU WILL KEEP HIM IN PERFECT PEACE, WHOSE MIND
IS STAYED ON YOU, BECAUSE HE TRUSTS IN YOU."

When you trust God with your future, you are less likely to worry. Although things may seem bleak, just remember that God has a wonderful future in store for you.

Reflection: **What do you desire from God?**

_____

_____

_____

_____

_____

Affirmation: **I will trust God!**

Confirmation: **"Trust in the Lord with all your heart, and lean not on your own understanding." Proverbs 3:5**

_____

_____

_____

_____

_____

_____

_____

We would all experience less stress if we perceived our mistakes as results instead of failures. We all fall short of our goals at times, but when we accept our shortcomings positively, we can achieve better results the next time.

Reflection: **How have your shortcomings helped you make better decisions?**

_____

_____

_____

_____

_____

Affirmation: **I can overcome!**

_____

_____

_____

_____

_____

_____

_____

_____

Are there small opportunities that you have missed because you were waiting on that colossal one? Wait no longer. There is much to gain from small opportunities. They will prepare you for that BIG one.

Reflection: **What small-scale choices or opportunities have you missed out on? Are there any you can take advantage of now?**

_____

_____

_____

_____

_____

Affirmation: **I will cherish every opportunity!**

Confirmation: **"For where your treasure is, there your heart will be also." Matthew 6:21**

_____

_____

_____

_____

_____

_____

_____

JOHN 14:27
"PEACE I LEAVE WITH YOU; MY PEACE I GIVE TO YOU;
NOT AS THE WORLD GIVES DO I GIVE TO YOU. LET
NOT YOUR HEART BE TROUBLED, NEITHER LET IT
BE AFRAID."

Season 4

PERSONAL GROWTH

STICKING YOUR NECK OUT CAN BE ANXIETY-PRO-voking. However, you have to take a chance to make progress. Like a tortoise, your progress may be slow and steady, but you must keep moving forward to win the race.

Reflection: **How has taking a risk or a chance benefited you in the past?**

_____

_____

_____

_____

_____

Affirmation: **No risk, no growth!**

Confirmation: **"I know your works. See, I have set before you an open door, and no one can shut it." Revelation 3:8**

_____

_____

_____

_____

_____

Nobody is holding you back but you. Excuses can handicap and cause you to be a prisoner to your fears. Identify someone who can hold you accountable for your excuses, and say to yourself, "No more limitations."

Reflection: **What are your excuses? Do you have an accountability partner? Is there anyone you can think of who could fill such a role in your life?**

_____

_____

_____

_____

_____

Affirmation: **I will accept accountability!**

_____

_____

_____

_____

_____

_____

_____

_____

_____

Nurture your strengths and watch them grow!

Reflection: **What are some of your strengths? How can you improve them further? How can they benefit you in moving forward?**

_____

_____

_____

_____

_____

Affirmation: **I will stay disciplined!**

Confirmation: **"Seek the Lord and His strength; Seek His face ever-more!" 1 Chronicles 16:11**

_____

_____

_____

_____

_____

_____

_____

_____

_____

ROMANS 8:37
"WE ARE MORE THAN CONQUERORS THROUGH HIM
WHO LOVED US."

Poor choices can lead to a lifetime of guilt. Pick up the pieces and begin the process of rebuilding your life.

Reflection: **Are there any past mistakes you still struggle to forgive yourself for today? How might you work on moving past these regrets?**

_____

_____

_____

_____

_____

Affirmation: **Challenges can make me stronger!**

Confirmation: **"And whatever things you ask in prayer, believing, you will receive." Matthew 21:22**

_____

_____

_____

_____

_____

_____

_____

Let persistence drive your hunger for growth!

Reflection: **What can you be more persistent about this week? List three things that can fuel your hunger for growth.**

_____

_____

_____

_____

_____

Affirmation: **Growth is birthed from persistence!**

_____

_____

_____

_____

_____

_____

_____

_____

_____

_____

You have much to offer this world. Don't diminish your self-worth by not pursuing your dreams. You are a rare gem. The world will be a better place because of your contributions.

Reflection: **What can you do to improve your self-worth?**

_____

_____

_____

_____

_____

Affirmation: **I will not cheat the world of my ideas!**

Confirmation: **"And the Lord will make you the head and not the tail; you shall be above only, and not be beneath." Deuteronomy 28:13**

_____

_____

_____

_____

_____

_____

_____

ROMANS 8:31
"IF GOD IS FOR US, WHO CAN BE AGAINST US?"

Time is valuable! Focus on activities that will benefit you for the rest of your life.

Reflection: **How are you managing your time? How can you improve your time management skills?**

_____

_____

_____

_____

Affirmation: **I will prune off meaningless activities!**

Confirmation: **"Go to the ant, you sluggard! Consider her ways and be wise." Proverbs 6:6**

_____

_____

_____

_____

_____

_____

_____

Have you ever been told that you have more "book sense" than common sense? Or that you're smart with little ambition? If so, then you're familiar with the feelings these statements can give rise to—feelings of inadequacy, regret, and fear. But above it all, God whispers and reminds you that you are created in His image. Listen to God's voice, not man's judgment.

Reflection: **How are you dealing with your insecurities? What do you need to change to break the chains of self-doubt?**

_____

_____

_____

_____

_____

Affirmation: **God loves me despite my limitations!**

_____

_____

_____

_____

_____

_____

_____

Faith and works propel you to heights beyond your imagination. Just believe; God will never fail you!

Reflection: **Do you believe in yourself? What do you need to propel yourself forward?**

_____

_____

_____

_____

_____

Affirmation: **God has my back!**

_____

_____

_____

_____

_____

_____

_____

_____

1 Peter 2:9
"But you are a chosen generation, a royal priesthood, a holy nation, His own special people, that you may proclaim the praises of Him who called you out of darkness into His marvelous light."

People-pleasing is burdensome. It steals your joy and peace. Choose to make decisions that please God instead, and you will reap great rewards.

Reflection: **Are you a people-pleaser? What steps can you take to change from a people-pleaser to a God-pleaser?**

_____

_____

_____

_____

_____

Affirmation: **I will make Spirit-led decisions!**

Confirmation: **"Teach me to do Your will, for You are my God; Your Spirit is good." Psalm 143:10**

_____

_____

_____

_____

_____

_____

_____

_____

You can either have a victim mentality or a victor mentality. Which do you choose? Don't be a prisoner of your victimization. You are a survivor! Celebrate all of your accomplishments—even small victories.

Reflection: **What type of mentality controls you? How can you improve or change this mentality?**

_____

_____

_____

_____

_____

Affirmation: **I am a victor!**

_____

_____

_____

_____

_____

_____

_____

_____

_____

_____

Character speaks volumes. It is even more important than what you do. Build your character, and success will follow.

Reflection: **What story are you telling with your character?**

_____

_____

_____

_____

_____

Affirmation: **I will put character first!**

Confirmation: **"He who walks with integrity walks securely, but he who perverts his ways will become known." Proverbs 10:9**

_____

_____

_____

_____

_____

_____

_____

_____

Would you consider yourself a giver who attracts takers? Have you observed that when you need someone, no one seems to be there for you? Take a few minutes to acknowledge your feelings. Now ask yourself, "What am I going to do differently to break this cycle?"

Reflection: **What ideas did you identify to break the cycle? How do you feel now?**

_____

_____

_____

_____

_____

Affirmation: **I value me!**

_____

_____

_____

_____

_____

_____

_____

_____

1 JOHN 1:9
"IF WE CONFESS OUR SINS, HE IS FAITHFUL AND JUST TO FORGIVE US OUR SINS AND TO CLEANSE US FROM ALL UNRIGHTEOUSNESS."

In spite of what many might think, we have all attended our own pity parties. For some of us, they lasted a few hours or days, but for others, they became a part of our lives. The key is to not remain at the pity party. Transform your pity into problem-solving so that you can receive help, hope, and happiness.

Reflection: **What's causing you to have pity parties? How can you use your pity as a motivation to solve a problem?**

_____

_____

_____

_____

_____

Affirmation: **No more pity parties!**

_____

_____

_____

_____

_____

_____

_____

It can be difficult to decide which conflicts to address or ignore. However, weighing the benefits and consequences of each decision can help. If you struggle with the need to be right and find yourself driven to fight every battle, ask God for the wisdom to know what to overlook to be at peace.

Reflection: **What conflicts can you ignore without them causing you too much stress?**

_____

_____

_____

_____

_____

Affirmation: **I will learn to choose my battles!**

Confirmation: **"The discretion of a man makes him slow to anger, and his glory is to overlook a transgression." Proverbs 19:11**

_____

_____

_____

_____

_____

_____

_____

2 CORINTHIANS 4:8–9

"WE ARE HARD-PRESSED ON EVERY SIDE, YET NOT CRUSHED; WE ARE PERPLEXED, BUT NOT IN DESPAIR; PERSECUTED, BUT NOT FORSAKEN; STRUCK DOWN, BUT NOT DESTROYED."

Season 5

SUCCESS

As you climb the pinnacle of success, you will face the reconstruction of your dreams, goals, and desires. Keep constructing—your empire is almost built!

Reflection: **What are your goals at this stage of your life? Have they changed as you have matured and progressed?**

_____

_____

_____

_____

_____

Affirmation: **I construct my pathway of success!**

Confirmation: **"Commit your works to the LORD, and your thoughts will be established." Proverbs 16:3**

_____

_____

_____

_____

_____

You were born to be unique, so begin to accept that "standing out" is good.

Reflection: **When you think of your uniqueness, what makes you smile? Write a few words that describe your uniqueness.**

_____

_____

_____

_____

_____

Affirmation: **I am unique!**

Confirmation: **"Before I formed you in the womb I knew you; before you were born I sanctified you; I ordained you a prophet to the nations." Jeremiah 1:5**

_____

_____

_____

_____

_____

_____

_____

PSALM 37:4
"DELIGHT YOURSELF ALSO IN THE LORD, AND HE
SHALL GIVE YOU THE DESIRES OF YOUR HEART."

Self-empowerment is success minus doubts and fears!

Reflection: **How have your doubts and fears made you stronger and brought you success?**

_____

_____

_____

_____

Affirmation: **No more emotional baggage!**

_____

_____

_____

_____

_____

_____

_____

_____

_____

Your success is determined by your choices, and your choices determine your destiny. Let your future be fueled by a lifetime of healthy choices.

Reflection: **How has your decision-making shaped your success?**

_____

_____

_____

_____

_____

Affirmation: **I determine my destiny!**

Confirmation: **"O LORD, You are the portion of my inheritance and my cup; You maintain my lot." Psalm 16:5**

_____

_____

_____

_____

_____

_____

_____

_____

_____

Don't settle for less! It is never too late to realize your dreams.

Reflection: **What do you value that defines your destiny?**

_____

_____

_____

_____

_____

Affirmation: **I am above average!**

_____

_____

_____

_____

_____

_____

_____

_____

_____

_____

PSALM 37:23
"THE STEPS OF A GOOD MAN ARE ORDERED BY THE LORD, AND HE DELIGHTS IN HIS WAY."

Strive for excellence, even when discouragement and despair whisper that you can't.

Reflection: **What stops you from striving for excellence?**

_____

_____

_____

_____

_____

Affirmation: **I will excel!**

Confirmation: **"But seek first the kingdom of God and His righteousness, and all these things shall be added to you." Matthew 6:33**

_____

_____

_____

_____

_____

_____

_____

_____

Prayer, patience, and perseverance are the keys to mastering difficulties in your life. There are opportunities to be won—you just have to do your part.

Reflection: **What do you need, personally, to master your challenges?**

_____

_____

_____

_____

Affirmation: **I will pray more, be patient, and persevere!**

_____

_____

_____

_____

_____

_____

_____

Success in contentious moments is when you use silence to tame the words that would bring deep regrets if they were said in anger.

Reflection: **Was there a time when anger resulted in severe consequences or severed relationships? How can you begin to practice the discipline of silence?**

_____

_____

_____

_____

_____

Affirmation: **I will value silence!**

Confirmation: **"Whoever guards his mouth and tongue keeps his soul from troubles." Proverbs 21:23**

_____

_____

_____

_____

_____

_____

_____

PHILIPPIANS 1:6
"BEING CONFIDENT OF THIS VERY THING, THAT HE WHO HAS BEGUN A GOOD WORK IN YOU WILL COMPLETE IT UNTIL THE DAY OF JESUS CHRIST."

Season 6

MENTAL & PHYSICAL HEALTH

FOR MANY YEARS, SCIENCE HAS REVEALED A DIS-connect between the mind and the body. Now more than ever, researchers believe that disease cannot be fully treated until there is an examination of the mind, body, and spirit.[1] Here is a start to you focusing on your whole person.

Reflection: **What does whole health mean to you? What is necessary for you to achieve or maintain whole health?**

_____

_____

_____

_____

Affirmation: **I will focus on my whole being!**

Confirmation: **"Beloved, I pray that you may prosper in all things and be in health, just as your soul prospers." 3 John 1:2**

_____

_____

_____

_____

_____

When you take the time to smell the roses, you will begin to manage your stress more effectively. Making an effort to slow down is challenging for some of us. (Type A's, you know what I mean.) Nevertheless, there is a great relief when you take fifteen to twenty minutes to slow down. So try it today and make a difference in your lifestyle.

Reflection: **What makes it difficult for you to slow your pace?**

_____

_____

_____

_____

_____

Affirmation: **It is okay to slow down!**

Confirmation: **"Come to Me, all you who labor and are heavy laden, and I will give you rest." Matthew 11:28**

_____

_____

_____

_____

_____

_____

_____

PSALM 29:11
"THE LORD WILL GIVE STRENGTH TO HIS PEOPLE;
THE LORD WILL BLESS HIS PEOPLE WITH PEACE."

Avoid chronic worry. It can cause insomnia, skin breakouts, and hair loss, sap your energy and cause anxiety and depression. Decide today to limit your worry to a "worry period."[2] I imagine you are asking yourself right now, "What is a worry period?" It's a period of time, usually twenty to thirty minutes when you give yourself permission to worry, solve problems, and then let it go.

Reflection: **How can you be intentional about your "worry period"?**

_____

_____

_____

_____

_____

Affirmation: **I will worry less!**

Confirmation: **"Casting all your care upon Him, for He cares for you." 1 Peter 5:7**

_____

_____

_____

_____

_____

_____

_____

Fear can cause you to become physically ill if it continues to reside in your soul. You are going to make mistakes, and it's okay. Life is not perfect!

Reflection: **How can you prevent fear from paralyzing you?**

_____

_____

_____

_____

_____

Affirmation: **Making mistakes does not make me a failure!**

Confirmation: **"Fear not, for I am with you; Be not dismayed, for I am your God. I will strengthen you, Yes, I will help you, I will uphold you with My righteous right hand." Isaiah 41:10**

_____

_____

_____

_____

_____

_____

_____

Fitness involves eating well and exercising regularly. Many people dislike exercising and have difficulty being consistent with it. The most common hindrance is making excuses such as "I don't have time" or "I'm in pain." Instead of making excuses, say *I will*, and *I can* instead.

Reflection: **What excuses hinder you from regular exercise and healthy eating? Identify one or two *I can* or *I will* statements that will foster a strong commitment to better health.**

Affirmation: **I will commit to being fit!**

ISAIAH 1:19
"IF YOU ARE WILLING AND OBEDIENT, YOU SHALL EAT
THE GOOD OF THE LAND."

Are you spending most of your time inside your house or office and not making time to enjoy a breath of fresh air? Research indicates that fresh air has many health benefits, such as cleansing toxins from your lungs, strengthening your immune system, and increasing your energy.[3] Commit to spending more time outside, preferably away from the city, and enjoy a healthier lifestyle.

Reflection: **What changes do you need to make so that you can enjoy the outdoors? Identify four outdoor activities that you really enjoy.**

_____

_____

_____

_____

_____

Affirmation: **I will commit to a daily breath of fresh air!**

_____

_____

_____

_____

_____

_____

_____

Aromatic baths are medicinal!
Think of times when you felt distressed or experienced considerable muscle or joint tension and took a nice hot aromatic bath. It provided the soothing relief you needed. Right? Never underestimate the power of water and essential oils.

Reflection: **What are some ways to improve your aromatherapy experience? List three essential oils that can further enhance your mental and physical well-being.**

_____

_____

_____

_____

_____

Affirmation: **Aromatherapy is a holistic approach that relaxes my mind and body.**

_____

_____

_____

_____

_____

_____

In the summer months, I enjoy spending a moderate amount of time in the sun. It brightens my mood, soothes my soul, and relaxes me. As you can imagine, the winters are challenging with shorter daylight hours, but I am intentional about keeping my home and office blinds open for those wonderful beams of sunlight. Join me and commit to sunshine daily.

Reflection: **What changes must you make to maximize the benefits of sunlight?**

_____

_____

_____

_____

_____

Affirmation: **I will take a "sun" moment!**

Confirmation: **"He grows green in the sun, and his branches spread out in his garden." Job 8:16**

_____

_____

_____

_____

_____

_____

In my clinical experience, many recovering addicts would often testify that it took them becoming sick and tired of doing drugs and hitting rock bottom for them to finally quit. Change is not easy, but it is doable when you depend on your higher power and are determined.

Reflection: **Are you sick and tired of your dysfunctional cycle? How can you begin a healthy recovery?**

_____

_____

_____

_____

_____

Affirmation: **I can make healthy lifestyle changes!**

_____

_____

_____

_____

_____

_____

_____

_____

When loneliness strikes, seek pure and creative forms of companionship and develop positive perceptions about loneliness.

Reflection: **How can you cope differently with loneliness? How might you learn to enjoy your own company?**

_____

_____

_____

_____

Affirmation: **Loneliness is no longer a foe of my life!**

Confirmation: **"I will not leave you nor forsake you." Joshua 1:5**

_____

_____

_____

_____

_____

_____

_____

_____

When you find yourself suddenly crying for no apparent reason, or you are overwhelmed with melancholy feelings, consider whether this is a time of the year when you have previously experienced significant trauma or losses.

Reflection: **What sad or traumatic anniversaries do you need to acknowledge so you can cope more effectively?**

_____

_____

_____

_____

_____

Affirmation: **Grieving matters!**

_____

_____

_____

_____

_____

_____

_____

_____

PSALM 103:12
"As far as the east is from the west, so far has He removed our transgressions from us."

Season 7

REST & RELAXATION

WE SOMETIMES TAKE FOR GRANTED THE SIGNIFI-
cance of rest until we begin to face stress-related diseases. Rest helps
us to slow down and become more in tune with our minds and bodies.
Take a moment and give yourself the gift of rest.

Reflection: **How can you have a day of rest?**

_____

_____

_____

_____

_____

Affirmation: **I will rest consistently!**

Confirmation: **"So the people rested on the seventh day." Exodus 16:30**

_____

_____

_____

_____

_____

When we are so focused on keeping busy, we sometimes miss out on life's simple pleasures. While busyness can serve as a positive distraction and keep you out of trouble (can I hear an "amen"?), you can also exhaust yourself to the point that you miss the simpler things in life.

Reflection: **What changes are you willing to make to enjoy the simple things in life?**

_____

_____

_____

_____

_____

Affirmation: **I will appreciate simplicity!**

_____

_____

_____

_____

_____

_____

_____

_____

_____

In this world of shutdowns and layoffs, taking a vacation is still a luxury for many. However, if you do not make time for yourself and your family, you will miss out on precious moments that you can never regain. A vacation from your day-to-day stressors will positively impact your health. Please make an effort to take some time off; you deserve it.

Reflection: **What lifestyle changes do you need to make so that taking a vacation becomes a reality and not just a fantasy?**

_____

_____

_____

_____

_____

Affirmation: **I will learn to relax!**

Confirmation: **"So they departed to a deserted place in the boat by themselves." Mark 6:32**

_____

_____

_____

_____

_____

_____

_____

PSALM 46:10
"BE STILL, AND KNOW THAT I AM GOD."

Studies have shown that laughter and sleep can lower your blood pressure, reduce stress, decrease depression, improve memory, and boosts creativity.[1] Heal yourself with the medicine of laughter and rest.

Reflection: **How can you ensure that you get a good night's sleep and a dose of laughter every day?**

_____

_____

_____

_____

_____

Affirmation: **I will laugh and rest!**

Confirmation: **"A merry heart does good, like medicine, but a broken spirit dries the bones." Proverbs 17:22**

_____

_____

_____

_____

_____

_____

_____

You will experience less stress if you take fifteen minutes for yourself.[2] Go for a walk, read a book or listen to some calming music. As you read this, you might be thinking, "I don't have fifteen minutes to spare." Ok, then compromise and take five minutes. Whatever you do, make a point of relaxing today.

Reflection: **How can you make relaxation a priority?**

_____

_____

_____

_____

Affirmation: **I will make time for me!**

_____

_____

_____

_____

_____

_____

_____

1 CORINTHIANS 6:19–20
"DO YOU NOT KNOW THAT YOUR BODY IS THE TEMPLE
OF THE HOLY SPIRIT WHO IS IN YOU, WHOM YOU HAVE
FROM GOD, AND YOU ARE NOT YOUR OWN? FOR YOU
WERE BOUGHT AT A PRICE; THEREFORE GLORIFY
GOD IN YOUR BODY AND IN YOUR SPIRIT, WHICH
ARE GOD'S."

Season 8

CHANGE

MANY PEOPLE HAVE DIFFICULTY LETTING GO OF the things they cannot change. Maybe you are one of them. This could be due to a need to control everything or a strong attachment to people or things. It is essential to identify the reasons we resist change and be determined to let go of what we cannot control.

Reflection: **What is causing you to hold on to situations that you cannot change?**

_____

_____

_____

_____

Affirmation: **I will let go of things I cannot change!**

Confirmation: **"Be anxious for nothing, but in everything by prayer and supplication, with thanksgiving, let your requests be made known to God." Philippians 4:6**

_____

_____

_____

_____

There is security in performing the same actions and expecting the same results. Ultimately, this leads to becoming complacent and stagnant, which inhibits personal growth. It is never too late to make a change.

Reflection: **What would it take for you to make significant changes to your life and routines?**

_____

_____

_____

_____

_____

Affirmation: **I will accept that change can be good!**

_____

_____

_____

_____

_____

_____

_____

_____

The past is the past. Sometimes we wish we could go back and make different decisions, but this will not help. However, working through the guilt and disappointments can motivate you to move forward to a brighter future. Free yourself of the past and begin a "change" reaction.

Reflection: **What is causing you to be stuck in the past?**

_____

_____

_____

_____

_____

Affirmation: **I will look forward to the future!**

Confirmation: **"A man's heart plans his way, but the Lord directs his steps." Proverbs 16:9**

_____

_____

_____

_____

_____

_____

_____

HEBREWS 10:23
"LET US HOLD FAST THE CONFESSION OF OUR HOPE
WITHOUT WAVERING, FOR HE WHO PROMISED IS
FAITHFUL."

It is sometimes easier to make a difference in others' lives than to change your own. Looking at one's ugly side is not easy. Choosing avoidance or denial as a way to cope only exacerbates the chaos. Change can be monumental!

Reflection: **What makes it difficult for you to change your world?**

_____

_____

_____

_____

Affirmation: **I can change my world with God's help!**

Confirmation: **"He who is in you is greater than he who is in the world." 1 John 4:4**

_____

_____

_____

_____

_____

_____

_____

Doing what is right can be challenging when it involves change. Most individuals want to follow the status quo. However, if you are convinced about doing what is morally correct, then do the right thing and initiate a change.

Reflection: **How can you begin to initiate a change that goes against the status quo?**

Affirmation: **I will have integrity!**

Are you so busy ministering to others that you miss spending time with God?

Reflection: **What changes must you make to spend quality time with the Lord?**

_____

_____

_____

_____

_____

_____

Affirmation: **I will dedicate more time to God!**

Confirmation: **"Now in the morning, having risen a long while before daylight, He went out and departed to a solitary place; and there He prayed." Mark 1:35**

_____

_____

_____

_____

_____

PSALM 121:8
"THE LORD SHALL PRESERVE YOUR GOING OUT AND YOUR COMING IN, FROM THIS TIME FORTH, AND EVEN FOREVERMORE."

Season 9
GRATITUDE & JOY

A WALK IN THE PARK, A PET CUDDLING NEAR YOUR side, and the aromatic scent of a flower all open our hearts to a sense of gratitude. Appreciate the little things in life!

Reflection: **What can you do to further appreciate the little things in life?**

_____

_____

_____

_____

_____

Affirmation: **It's the little things that matter!**

Confirmation: **"But those who seek the Lord shall not lack any good thing." Psalm 34:10**

_____

_____

_____

_____

_____

What is on your gratitude channel? Tune into love and compassion.

Reflection: **How can you tune more into gratitude? Identify four things you are most grateful for today.**

_____

_____

_____

_____

_____

Affirmation: **I will turn on my gratitude!**

Confirmation: **"Oh, give thanks to the Lord, for He is good! For His mercy endures forever." Psalm 107:1**

_____

_____

_____

_____

_____

_____

_____

_____

_____

Feed gratitude and kindness will grow.

Reflection: **What positive outcomes have you experienced from embracing gratitude?**

_____

_____

_____

_____

_____

Affirmation: **I choose to be kind!**

_____

_____

_____

_____

_____

_____

_____

_____

_____

MATTHEW 6:34
"THEREFORE, DO NOT WORRY ABOUT TOMORROW, FOR
TOMORROW WILL WORRY ABOUT ITS OWN THINGS.
SUFFICIENT FOR THE DAY IS ITS OWN TROUBLE."

Researchers have discovered that expressing gratitude can improve mood.[1] Think about a time you felt sad or hurt, and someone expressed their appreciation. Didn't you feel better? Bring more joy into life by practicing gratitude.

Reflection: **How has gratitude improved your attitude or mood?**

_____

_____

_____

_____

_____

Affirmation: **More gratitude, more joy!**

Confirmation: **"Rejoice always, pray without ceasing, in everything give thanks; for this is the will of God in Christ Jesus for you." 1 Thessalonians 5:16–18**

_____

_____

_____

_____

_____

_____

Simple words such as "thank you" can dispel tension. It is wonderful to see a positive change just by showing appreciation. Gratitude can motivate others to change!

Reflection: **What changes have you made in your behavior as a result of gratitude?**

_____

_____

_____

_____

_____

Affirmation: **I will impact other's behavior with gratitude!**

_____

_____

_____

_____

_____

_____

_____

_____

_____

ISAIAH 46:11
"INDEED, I HAVE SPOKEN IT; I WILL ALSO BRING IT TO
PASS. I HAVE PURPOSED IT; I WILL ALSO DO IT."

Discontentment can destroy your happiness. Learn to be content, and you will experience the greatest joy and peace.

Reflection: **What can you do to increase your personal contentment?**

_____

_____

_____

_____

_____

Affirmation: **I will let go of discontentment!**

Confirmation: **"For I have learned in whatever state I am, to be content." Philippians 4:11**

_____

_____

_____

_____

_____

_____

_____

Sometimes all it takes is a smile. Smiling reduces physical and emotional tension.[2] Smile regularly, and you will feel better. Not only will your smile affect you, but also others. Keep smiling!

Reflection: **How has your smile been a blessing to others?**

_____

_____

_____

_____

_____

Affirmation: **Smiling makes a difference!**

_____

_____

_____

_____

_____

_____

_____

_____

_____

Joy can be contagious.[3] Spread your joy! Make the world a better place.

Reflection: **How can your joy be contagious? List six ways you can spread joy.**

_____

_____

_____

_____

_____

Affirmation: **My heart is filled with joy!**

Confirmation: **"The joy of the Lord is your strength." Nehemiah 8:10**

_____

_____

_____

_____

_____

_____

_____

_____

We tend to think that we need people or things in our lives to be happy. However, true happiness comes from God. He knows how to transform your happiness into joy. Let go of those things you thought you needed, and let God give you everlasting joy.

Reflection: **How has God given you eternal joy?**

_____

_____

_____

_____

_____

Affirmation: **My joy comes from God!**

_____

_____

_____

_____

_____

_____

_____

_____

PHILIPPIANS 4:4–5
"REJOICE IN THE LORD ALWAYS. AGAIN I WILL
SAY, REJOICE! LET YOUR GENTLENESS BE KNOWN
TO ALL MEN."

NOTES

Preface

1. Pennebaker JW. *Opening up: The healing power of expressing emotions.* New York, NY: Guilford Press; 1990.

2. Smyth J. Written emotional expression: Effect sizes, outcome types, and moderating variables. *Journal of Consulting and Clinical Psychology.* 1998; 66(1):174–184.

Season 1

1. Kleingeld A, van Mierlo H, Arends L. The effect of goal setting on group performance: A meta-analysis. *Journal of Applied Psychology.* 2011; 96(6):1289-1304.

2. Petrocchi N, Ottaviani C, Couyoumdjian A. Compassion at the mirror: Exposure to a mirror increases the efficacy of a self-compassion manipulation in enhancing soothing positive affect and heart rate variability. *The Journal of Positive Psychology.* 2017;12(6): 525-536.doi: 10.1080/17439760.2016.1209544.

3. Beck JS. *Cognitive therapy: Basics and beyond.* New York, NY: Guilford Press; 1995.

Season 6

1. Leitan ND, Murray G. The mind-body relationship in psychotherapy: Grounded cognition as an explanatory framework. *Frontiers in Psychiatry.* 2014; 5(472):69-76.

2. Borkovec TD, Wilkinson L, Folensbee R, Lerman C. Stimulus control applications to the treatment of worry. *Behaviour Research and Therapy.* 1983; 21(3):247-251.

3. Sarris J, de Manincor M, Hargraves F, Tsonis J. Harnessing the Four Elements for Mental Health. *Frontiers in Psychiatry.* 2019;10 (3389):256.

Season 7

1. King B. *The Laughing Cure: Emotional and Physical Healing? A Comedian reveals Why Laughter Really Is the Best Medicine.* New York, NY: Skyhorse; 2016.

2. Pascoe MC, Thompson, Jenkins ZM, Ski CF. Mindfulness mediates the physiological markers of stress: Systematic review and meta-analysis. Jou*rnal of Psychiatric Research. 2017*; 95 (1016):156-178.

Season 9

1. Emmons RA, Crumpler CA. Gratitude as a human strength: Appraising the evidence. *Journal of Social and Clinical Psychology.* 2000; 9:56-69.

2. Kraft TL, Pressman SD. Grin and bear it: The influence of manipulated facial expression on the stress response. *Psychological Science.* 2012;23(11):1372-1378.

3. Christakis NA. Dynamic spread of happiness in a large social network: Longitudinal analysis over 20 years in the Framingham Heart Study. *BMJ.* 2008; 337:a2338.

ROMANS 15:13
"NOW MAY THE GOD OF HOPE FILL YOU WITH ALL JOY
AND PEACE IN BELIEVING THAT YOU MAY ABOUND IN
HOPE BY THE POWER OF THE HOLY SPIRIT."

APPENDIX

Dear Journaler-Reader,

I would be remiss if I didn't acknowledge that *Who Cares? A Guided Self-Help & Devotional Journal for the Seasons of Life* is being published during one of the worst pandemics to cross the globe and cause millions of deaths.

My heart hurts for so many that have lost loved ones to COVID-19. Grief can be a complicated and painful process. It's a journey with an outcome only you can determine. I have created a compilation of resources that can assist you with navigating the journey through grief.

If you would like a copy, please email me at whocaresjournal@gmail.com

Grace & Peace,

Dr. Melita

PSALM 55:22
"CAST YOUR BURDEN ON THE LORD,
AND HE SHALL SUSTAIN YOU."

CPSIA information can be obtained
at www.ICGtesting.com
Printed in the USA
BVHW060906061022
648787BV00004B/103